Escaping the Timeline

Poems on Family, Karma and Boundaries

by Rebecca Trowbridge

For Nigel, Zoe and Maya

Copyright 2022 by Rebecca Trowbridge. All rights reserved.

This book or any portion thereof may not be reproduced or used in any manner whatsoever without the express written permission of the author except for the use of brief quotations in a book review or scholarly journal.

"Emperor Dragonfly flying male in Bahrenfeld, Hamburg" by Aiwok used by Rebecca Trowbridge under CC BY-SA 3.0 (https://creativecommons.org/licenses/by-sa/3.0/).
Contrast and brightness increased from the original located at https://commons.wikimedia.org/wiki/File:Anax_imperator_m1.JPG.
Cover design edited by Penny Creighton.

Acknowledgements

Gratitude and awe go to members of writers' groups (such as Hunter Writer's Centre) for their insight and skillful edits: Ann Clark, April Klasen, Bronwyn MacRitchie, Diana Pearce, Ellen Shelley, Jeanne Leppard, John Hingston, Lisa Barron, Maxine Jacobi, Megan Buxton, Nicole Sellers, Olivia Hamilton, Phil Williams, Trisha Green and Vicki MacDonald. Thank you, Kelly Alfris, April Klasen and Lou-Anne Page for your very much appreciated beta reader feedback. Thank you Milla Vlatko for cover design feedback.

Conversations sparked the muse from these inspiring people: Loreto Whitney, Catherine McCormack (who provided the last line in *Not Smothering to Bother With*), Catherine King, Lizzy Ehlies, Nichola Turenhout, April Young, Nikki Borgelt, Lauren Waldrom, Lou-Anne Page, Reina Stalker, Magdalena Ball and Shashona McCall. As always, I am indebted to my partner Nigel and our two wonderful girls for the adventure and experiences we share.

I acknowledge with respect the traditional custodians of the land I live and write on, the Awabakal people, and their elders, past, present, and emerging.

Deepest appreciation goes to mother earth for the continued rich teachings of the soul, and for those that travel with us on our paths.

Author Biography

Rebecca Trowbridge juggles law study, family and writing. She has spent time as an army corporal, geologist, market research caller, ski lodge manager, university tutor and high school teacher, while living and working around Australia from the outback to the coast. She has a Masters in Volcanology and wants you to know that lava flows downhill. Her other poetry collections include *Fossilised Lightning* and *Bitter Matriarch: Poems on Family, the Universe and Belonging*. Her other books, for young people, include *Cherry Chicken Chocolate Kitchen*, *Congraduations! You Finished!* and *Fond Farewells: Stories that Comfort when Saying Goodbye*.

http://rebeccatrowbridge.com/

Table of Contents

Family Snapshot

Compass 9

Spiny Leaf Insect 10

Royal Pain 12

My Daughter, the Insurrectionist 13

Getting Along with In-Laws 14

Post-Exorcism Damage Control 16

Insomnia Anyway 18

The Smell of Bread 19

Neuralgia 20

11 PM 22

Growing Up for the Children

First Time Cook 25

A Dream Where I Meet Repressed Rage 26

First to Outgrow 27

Literary Scene 29

Retreat 30

Welcome to your beautiful stream 31

Internal Crisis 34

Don't Rescue.   The Desert is Infinite Potential Energy 36

Cthulu 38

Rope Fell Out of the Sewing Box 40

Ri(f)t 41

Four Seasons Toward Self-Love 42

Hoodoo Rocks 46

Obligations and Torture at Christmas 48

Emotion-dumpers and Energy-feeders 50

Not Smothering to Bother With 52

Escaping the Timeline 55

Finding the Grace in Everything

Si(gh)t 59

Protecting the Blessings 60

Learning Integrity 62

Loose ends 64

Blue hands 66

Suspended 67

Viewing Drinkwater's Ocean Face Bronze 68

Lift 69

Viewing Ronald Ong's Heights 70

Marble Caves 72

Nudibranchs 74

G-force Nine 76

Dracaena Cinnabari 79

Lighting Incense to Ancestors 81

The Beaches Parkrun, Australia, December 84

Family Snapshot

Compass

They say dragonflies mean clarity
or they could mean illusion
but it had to mean something
opening the door
to the biggest one yet,
frozen in arrow pose,
stuck by mirror-ball eyes
to fly screen at face-level.

G'day, buddy. You alright?

The bug-whisperer knew
to hold the noble darter
in her palm to the sun.
It buzzed, revved, rose and went
and the house felt humbled
that, as the moon frosted,
a troubled zip-spirit
pinned hope at this door.

Spiny Leaf Insect

When my daughter got spiky,
Autumn seethed an electric hum;
flexed dorsal thorns.

For the right attitude,
it cycled two arms up for a lift
to climb bouncy-castle skin.

It has since settled disputes
between siblings
spurning spikes for the gentler mood

no matter how strong
the aggrieved party's case
pleading trespass to Lego.

It has ascended in rank
from pet and curiosity
to wise judge, oracle and healer.

When it clatters, dead-leafed, to tiles,
we ponder Transience of Being
and prod the One Most High to life.

We serve Its Eminence gum leaves,
face the perch to White Tiger West
and sweep its sacred droppings.

We bow greetings each morning
to its venerable sageness
hung upside down, splayed backward,

and pray to master, this lifetime,
one curl of the little phasmid's
yogic divinity.

Royal Pain

Father, daughter, bicker, bait;
tussles for power fascinate.
I am the queen. I choose to eat cake.

Children wail *MumMumIwantyou*;
Husband insists on his stories too.
I am the queen. Form an orderly queue.

Manners cost nothing. I refuse
to accept disrespect and uncouth.
I am the queen. I will ignore you.

Boundaries mean preserving my peace.
I can't let your conflicts in turn infect me.
I must be queen. I keep sipping my tea.

My Daughter, the Insurrectionist

At six,

ladylike,

she won't

flip the

middle

finger,

but draw

them—

all sizes

per her

feelings,

with nail

polish—

then watch

me closely

as she says

Mummy,

Look at this.

Getting Along with In-Laws

Careful conduct ends the feud:
be polite, use eye contact,
close my mouth, chew my food,

plot exits—a multitude—
keep my social space intact;
careful conduct ends the feud.

Smile and say some platitude.
When I tire as diplom-act,
close my mouth. Chew my food.

If they slip with something rude,
prompt them with some gentle tact.
Careful conduct ends the feud—

since they too hope wars conclude,
keep the truce's prudent pact—
close my mouth. Chew my food.

Note their mirrored attitude:

seeing me, they don't react.

Careful conduct ends the feud:

close my mouth. Chew, chew, chew.

Post-Exorcism Damage Control

We had a chat so she'd know about:

>permission, boundaries, respect;
>that psychic tools are a last resort
>because your voice is powerful
>so learn courage and use it;

>if you interfere with people,
>you'll end up with their karma
>but if they directly affect you,
>okay, do what you gotta do;

which I cover in 15 minutes
including quiz scenarios

apparently sucking air out of the car
so she promises to mind her own business

but I'll keep an eye on that one
though she's a good kid and honestly

if my sister was burping and laughing
me awake after a big day

I'd flame up the little demon too.

Insomnia Anyway

I could have handled it better
like many other things.
I needed sleep
after a long week
and the kids bickered all evening

and perhaps on another day
I might have kept in their room,
chosen kinder explanations
for the door that swung itself
as the eldest settled in

but "It's just your Grandpa,
and he spooked me too, at eight.
Scared me for decades. But not you
since you'll tell him
you don't appreciate that crap.

Now go on, go to bed."

The Smell of Bread

The neighbour's father argues
with some romeo from Tinder™
in the street.

I watch TV, *The Good Fight*,
but everyone's voices
start to compete.

I press my ear to the door;
verify it's them
and their language.

What will get rid of this?
Perhaps a kind scent.
Popcorn? Barbecued sausage?

I intend smells of fresh bread.
In the silence, I enjoy
the legal drama instead.

Neuralgia

The thing bites. Electric eel nerve, a wire frayed.
The paroxysm shocks from jaw to brain,
wraps the whole body around it.
He spasms, lashed for minutes.
It came true, his worst-case warning
each visit to high voltage:
Hit me with a plank
til I let go, if I get zapped,
he'd told every apprentice
stunned by sudden stakes.

This inside job means the body gone rogue;
surgery on the cause
did not relieve symptoms like
Pregabalin's side-effect suic/ide/as
and licking your lips trips the circuit
with loops: *When will it end?*
Be afraid of the lips.
Be afraid of the thought and lie still.
Absolutely still.

We tumble down the stairs,
morning-dragged
to Dad wrestling with his face.
The girls panic—*What's wrong?*
Dad's in tears, crawling—
the hiding spot from the kids' worry
is kicked over to exposure.
I yell, *Don't be useless, hold his hand for god's sake*
and they do, wailing, while he yells *Stop yelling!*
and Jordan Peterson on the TV says *Life is tragic,*
but you don't have to make it hellish.

11 PM

yield and drowse
lush exhaustion
heavy-limbed
round blankets, down-
soft whisper dark

wrapsafe, hum low
wavelets, calm let
glide   drop
plumb
.

.

red
L.E.Ds
dot the room
a moth bats wings
outside, mosquito squee
pub-crawl revelers call
car alarm

fridge jumps
headlights scan the room
gravel crunch, will they knock?
doors locked?

drip

caw

      creak

how much night-time?
mind-map tomorrow

      virus tests
      kids shots
      brain doctors
           fingers crossed
      lego sale

choose to trust
and I might sleep.

Growing Up for the Children

First Time Cook

I was lucky
(Mum started a lot younger)
at twelve, to cook dinners.
She showed me:
how to wash chicken,
set three bowls to dip
flour, egg, breadcrumbs;
rinse well the Chinese cress
 and submerge it in soup
or the broth became bitter;
soak dried shiitakes
overnight, season mince
with soy sauce, sugar
and cornflour, then fry
before steaming
in water-whisked eggs.
I was lucky to learn this
but my brother didn't have to.
It was my resentment
that would eat and grow fat.

A Dream Where I Meet Repressed Rage

I goad a man in black.
He smashes my head into bathroom mirrors
yet no blood.

Broken glass tinkles on white tiles.

The carbon smell of his lungs
fans my face,
his hands burn my throat.

First to Outgrow

We outgrow societal roles,
stop sacrifice to definition,
explore woods beyond the garden
through dark archways of trees,
a jungled path to epiphany,
and someone in the house
calls you back for reassurance
when you've gone ahead first.

Someone feels threatened
if you don't present, front and centre,
your familiar edges. The kitchen light
defines the limits of this life.
Or by the fence, they'll face forest,
then relief when you appear,
see you different, new, bigger
and keep the back light on, after.

The thickets shrink with every advance
while mapping self-expansion.
Do they wait for an old you? Or venture too?

Or deeply disappoint with ruins,
though burns birth the free spirit
you've always wanted to be
and prevent the return
to insecurity, once you.

Literary Scene

Tonight, my partner will stir mid-sleep and say my whole face is covered in moths. In the writing workshop, they shuttered my head from the hunt by a totem pole based on a trophy pact: prop someone on top, sit on someone else. But the stacking's a jostle. When the order's outgrown, the crown's unbalanced—crushes others looking up to them. Why do creatives crave esteem and give away their power by expressing inauthentic; choose words that seek to please? Take this moth-velvet mask, grey as background, to ghost. Disappear into truth between self and muse.

Retreat

The retreat brings sanctification when my subconscious reveals an eight-year-old, bags packed, with an announcement to run away and Mum agreed, pinning clothes to the line. The kid stayed, and I am in awe. She is about to cop life and I realise her resilience. Everything I am, was already within her. I kneel at her feet and hug the baffled girl. Healing spills raw ugly through a drowning room. We swim in deep vulnerability. We crack open, pluck ingrown shell from old sores—a hurt in reverse, a cellular purge, a soul explosion. *Now everyone find a partner and look in their eyes for two minutes*, improvises the convenor. I don't want to, but I fold; pliant, soft. Through blue eyes I see toy boats on a childhood pond and kindness, wringing me through a second baptism while I dare down the minutes, gritted. On the alarm I propel to shore after the convenor's push down a rockslide, susceptible to a bond, extorted after the transcendent connection to self. *Surrender to your spiritual master*, wrote an elder. I'm glad I braved the minutes, learned how boundaries weaken, but as everyone hugs out the last day, I burn tyres ascending the freeway.

Welcome to your beautiful stream

Through the window, a brilliance
vagues furniture.
Human figures, outlines blurred,
join hands in a ring.
You step back, wonder if you should run.
Oh, but the relief.

A cricket trills. A lull.
One friend in the hovering stillness
of night's mouth held open, waiting.
Possums scratch in trees,
eyes beacons by cabin.
Native mice skip through bracken.

Around the corner, a door,
a kitchen table where more sit.
Now inside light,
you feel solid,
colours vivid unlike
the incandescent ones.

Your body feels dense, entrenched.
You sense the stretch of skin
by pumps of blood and breath.
Your toes claw inside shoes.
An eyelash tickles your cheek.

Their faces nod toward you, slow,
like their speech: *Grace?* [musical, soft].
They offer palms, of course
you extend yours.
Fluorescence floods on touch,
rises. You, curious to shine,

stare. Worms pour from your chest—
twist, fall, dissolve—in light. You stare,
they unwind
thick segments from muscle,
force cloth ripples,
writhe frantic into air.

You realise you were screaming
once the flow trickles.

You realise you

did not break.

Someone nods at someone else.

We all have garbage to spill.

Internal Crisis

For those who thought heartbreak was pathetic, then had one.

When sun unlocks snow,
the bulk fleck-ice confronts
liquid chinks; a dilute self
undermines its own build
and flows chilling fallibility,
massed by melt-momentum's
               lost   solidity.

Water's weak internal bonds,
smashed on crags and
          cast from cliffs,
     rip the torrent
          to mist and froth
              to annihilate
     this instability

then the column
          collides,
thunders
         toward terrain

        for gushing's
           deliberate
     obliteration

but the tumult

unearths,

force tunnels

a bowl

that cups

clear

and

deep

    your   pool

   at   fall's

    end.

Beetles dig their hard shine into my palm,
along the heart line, for its juice.
Which dying—the little vampires or crossing dunes?
I choose walking. I might survive; learn faith.
Each step forces electric strikes by sand grains
through the soles into nerves; rewires the brain.
Soon flinted sparks surge spinal luminescence;
later flames ward off beetles
and sand fuses to glass mimicking sky.
The day, still dune-bound, gifts shimmer-pool tracks.
A path of death on a sunstroke-high.

Don't Rescue.

The Desert is Infinite Potential Energy.

One mirror-tread: ancient China,
I as a little lord and you as my favourite.
This mirage: Sparta and you, a soldier
bred with a proven child-bearer,
high-born. My husband envied our passion;
arranged an assassin.
Here: our teacher-student scandal

in Turkey—demonic possession.
There, our affair in post-Bonaparte France
but I never left my children nor the bad marriage.
In Russia as your sexpionage target, my arrogance
ignored warnings; I met God in torture.
I disguised as a man on our Portuguese merchant boat;
you died by pirate; I mended in Spain.
You were Norway seeking conquest and I,
Iceland fighting for sovereignty.
I trek, turn from each wraith, let go to free myself,
find true sustenance in a single tear:

Beyond time,

I remember

who I am.

Cthulu

Cthulu is a monstrous octopus
where patterns of stale relating jockey.

Endless tendrils tighten each grievance
make sticky ruts that trade our feelings
so *you* heave *their* grief—confused, exhausted
—while *they* feel neutral, but empty.

Cerebral networks thicken
in habits of thought and reaction –
old misunderstandings, blame
and conflict fire in a narrow range.

Reflection clears Cthulu's head
whose skin burst-peels, reveals water –
shed-ready tears we'll never need cry
once freed from emotional riptides.

The tears collapse to earth, disperse,
flush wrong resonance; no cosy sucking

on septic connections
to prop up the battle with self.

Cosmic neurons become light, flat, thin
and truth has clean, transparent links.

Rope Fell Out of the Sewing Box

One end frayed.
The well-worn cord cut short
made a small tail from
two loops bound by
twine turned twice
like a tether-go-round
as if in a brief adventure
we got caught in a vortex
before escaping each other
with scant time for progress.

Ri(f)t

Ri(gh)t

Four Seasons Toward Self-Love

In love they give out nothing of themselves, having no self to give, but enclose themselves around you in agonized reflection.
- Lawrence Durrell: *Justine*

Campers

must use the bush kitchen,

powered only by surplus from the house.

They bring their own food and clean up their mess

or get refused next visit. These are firm rules, she's had

trouble with pests. With her private key to the hearth fire

she wonders about guest comfort in the cooler months. As

a reply, one man takes his cereal to the balcony. Above

jewelled leaves sweetened brown, he crunches

his way through blood-orange floods

pouring dawn.

If I go above clouds
and magnetic shrouds,

would you flare up
or spare the scald?

If I walk on crystal rays
to your nuclear heart,

initiate myself, mirror
light from my palms;

if I match your eclipse,
would you let me in?

Politeness
goes in sleet and
snow. I trek to you,
not through blizzard
but from it. I hope for
fire but if no warmth,
a roof; or if shut out,
a wall. A wall means:
one direction I'm not
belted with hail, or
a shelter-prop,
a cryo-cocoon; as
even ice furies can
aid in a snow cave.
That's a comfort.
Perhaps.

*At night if
we heard rustles,
we wouldn't look but
jerk back to security.
Yet with illumination,
curiosity. Following a
huddled chill as earth
gave little, none resist
their own beauty; sing.
The unknown hides a
black panther
branch-draping its
self-assurance, eyes
on us in challenge:
find the same in
ourselves.*

Hoodoo Rocks

Mineral-mummified,
airstream-sculpted
grain by plucked grain,
only knobbled legs remain:
hoodoo columns remnant of
old ways to animate.

They were giants once,
sent lightning's jagged relief
through bones to earth
to ground and direct power.

You twist the posts like clockwork keys,
re-anchor rods, and hope for heaven
but I, soot-dry, combustible, shrunk,
galvanize a mere scent
of moonmilk crumbled.
Though still you love me,
you want me abundant.

I know other magic.
Let me lie in winters never ceasing
so snow and ash steep these bones
to petrify as opal
seep play-of-colour fire through seams
that stitch as veins through matrix.
No desert museum's
dessicate hoodoo
relic-sky magic
but soil-nested
smoulder-percolate
legacy.

Let this be my next invoking.
I cannot resurrect for you again.

Obligations and Torture at Christmas

She visited Saint Nicholas
(in prison by edict of Constantius:
believers to be beaten,
hauled away on wagons).
Conversation thinned
the centuries between them.
He told her he'd prayed but
God did not answer.
She said *Yes, I feel the same.*
Mum's making me visit
her cronies in nursing homes
as chauffeur all Christmas day.

They agreed they'd been
dutiful, but intrusion
by an authority meant doubts
they'd ever find peace
or acknowledgement,
consideration, even,
for being human
rather than a sacrifice.

Could they be left, instead,
to her dog and ten acres
or a diocese to oversee
not Evil Eye taxing kind natures?

They made a vow.
The arseholes wouldn't
pull them down
and both were getting out.
You know, you're a miracle
she said. Through the bars
he took her calloused hands
and wept.

Emotion-dumpers and Energy-feeders

The surf freshens goosebumps. We hope the salt heals us.
A relative swims to us, urinates, leaves us.

Ah. Trapped in this ocean of Oneness, we steep in
whatever gets dumped and the dumping blasphemes us.

Our protest makes urine a yellow top worn by
excreters who flee; thwarts those who disease us.

The waves twinkle everyone's true phosphorescence
in glimmers and flashes, the brightness redeems us.

But some of us hungry and parasites, needy,
drain life-force from contact: connection depletes us.

Or others tread water supporting their close ones
in turn feeding those who won't grow, which defeats us.

We're filtering mess in a psychic-fuel food chain,
enabling with bonds the bad conduct that cheats us.

Our energy's powering other agendas.
We're kept codependent and fear of truth bleeds us.

When jetties get swept out and boat harbours splinter,
withdraw to become rocky shores. Our strength frees us.

Let rocks hold the lighthouses steadily shining
without wading in to save ships. Light reveals us.

When centred in Self, retrieved life-force means soaring.
The winds flit new voices and scents. A dream seeks us.

Not Smothering to Bother With

I wonder how she is, my white aunt
with three brothers then three sons.
She and Mum never got along.

They should have, with their
competitive bent
for Alpha Woman.

I don't need a husband now, Mum said
when my brother was born.
He never really weaned off her.

She brags about the
transience of his girlfriends.
There's a policy, apparently.

No texts to prove love
and a use-by date of six months,
or the gold-diggers get half his money.

Too bad for all the women he went through,
who didn't know. Now in his forties,
he's trying with a fiancée

who Mum hates like the rest.
I've shut my door on that storm,
lightning grateful I'm not the favorite.

My partner's one of three boys, his mum's
resentment reserved for daughters-in-law,
the safest place for her negativity.

But like China regretting its girls-are-less culture,
there's a self-serving scramble
for connection with the feminine.

Thanks ladies, I parent my girls
as a process of letting go,
pass truth and encouragement.

I've no other home. I'm committed to this:
facing worst and best self in the kid-mirrors,
purging myself of emotional codependency.

Any other way means they'll lack
their own authority or self-respect,
run back to a childhood home to fix things,

too insecure for new beginnings,
or fatten egos on unconditional esteem,
and crippled, live small, risk-free.

They've got talents to practice
with adventures, self-discovery
not smothering to bother with.

They'll be so autonomous
as adults they could only partner
another grown-up.

My friend broke her heart to watch her son
walk his own path, a proud grief as he becomes
his own man. She and I will hang out as crones,

kids with full lives, leaving us alone.
They'll be so independent,
they forgot they had parents.

Escaping the Timeline

The adult version of learning
Santa's not real:
seeing the system wreak
an intricate challenge—
biology, society and beyond
pose inwrought flaws
to test tensile strength.
We must go within
to overcome, build
and drill discipline.

This is my fourth
run of this life;
foreshadows thick
and meant to remind:
born into deep
maternal misogyny,
Dad's midnight death with
our attempts to revive him
then his friend's predations
I'd fight year after year

despite crazy older people

with their own ordeals,

followed by

male-dominant careers

and quiet, toxic groups

with eggshell minefields

to program

red flags,

next

steps,

aversions,

rejections,

all the

tics

that drive

healing experiences,

spiritual mentors

mining jewels in dysfunction
for meaning in all facets
of painful events,
evolving skills
with supportive friends,
partner and liberator-children

all for a new awareness:

surviving two years of sustained psychic attacks
with mental, emotional and physical health intact
to cycle out this timeline and never come back.

Thank you, all.
It's done.

Finding the Grace in Everything

Si(gh)t

Si(f)t

Protecting the Blessings

Up in the chancel of Mont-Saint-Michel,
perching church on The Rock That Fell,
arrive in grace to a peaceful heart
lifted by pillars, horizons and glass.

Shored by the work to persist in the climb,
anchored by granite, the barricade isle
circled by tides is where one reclaims
sacredness, felt in the realm of the Saint.

Monks of the abbey of Mont-Saint-Michel
knew grace from labor and forts. And bells.
They were the barons of maritime trade,
mastered inherited commerce and gain:

bronze and bells, slate, salt and fish;
ruling the imports of copper and tin;
gathering taxes; controlling the passage,
keeps and ports each side of The Channel.

People need bells. The monks have to eat.
Money won't care if one's pirate or priest,
—both if a holy service to others is
cleverly leveraged to service oneself.

Centuries on, still the Mont draws wealth—
business is strong with visitor help:
communing with shops at the base of the rock;
joining the pious in song at the top.

Here where the worship is money and faith,
strength in defence is Saint Michel's grace
attracting to rapture in anchor-stone isles
with blessings protected by bulwarks and tides.

Learning Integrity

We think we know what's right and wrong
and choose the side of prosecution,
with black and white views
to round 'em up and burn 'em.

Until someone we know commits a crime.
We backflip – shock, then denial,
then the legal scheming,
make excuses, still disbelieving.
The bright apple snack is brown inside
—a warning of a flaw that finds reward
in winning puzzles and games,
a clever conceit to exploit
when there's guilt to avoid.

Reality fights with naïve concern.
Does knowing the whole person confuse us?
Do attachments detach our integrity?
Perhaps environmental law
is the path, perhaps courts

are compassionate enough:

let's withdraw to balance karma;

be neutral instead,

in our thoughts

Loose ends

There's unfinished business
in stories around me.

The magnate that murdered a black slave
to help a friend, then reborn, became
a black slave, and was slain
by one who became my husband
plagued by vague anxieties,
to support me, this life.

I've remembered the lesson:
stand in our own authority
and build our integrity—
our collective super-life's at stake.
Have discipline, don't take
what isn't ours—a life,
another's consequence.

That connection with selves
breaks fated causation;

my partner's guilt gone
in karmic acquittal.

Blue hands

Commitment distills in blue chalk
you hold for games with your children
dust your hands blue like in the dream
where you offered them up, patchy blue
and were told *Well done*

like an estranged husband in *The Abyss*
who threw his wedding ring in the toilet
rethought it, retrieved it, stained his arm
blue from disinfectant

and in *Immortel* another pulled his lover
up from a bath of blue tears
his arm also dyed; *Well done*

Suspended

The outcrop erodes; soil-thrown rocks and scree
drag a scar down the bank and two trees
though crown-shy, reveal at root their tryst;
the lower twining could not bind loose ground
and so they cling—bared bond by the precipice,
a suspended moment, perhaps weeks—
together at the edge of collapse into void,
lovers certain now not of earth but of the other
to hold them.

Viewing Drinkwater's *Ocean Face* Bronze

My fried eyes are devilled by the kindred dark form.
Its flesh melted to the bone.
There is barbecue in the room.
Burned? Nothing, the little ego croaks from its pedestal.
Your screen time is small bloody potatoes.
It glares, collateral of chemical warfare,
gravely dispraising my twin coddled yolks.

It drips fat as glazed pools wafting of braised stew;
a spattered pommel of a foil skewering sirloin;
juice-sheathed knuckles squeezing a shank of roast,
off sizzle.
Is that starfish garnish?
Perhaps star anise stuck in grease?
There, in primordial soup, glisten lizard phalanges:
a tiny meal of metatarsal tendons.

At the desk, I forgot myself.
Thanks for the reminder.
I distend my craw;
devour it all.

Lift

        Light

Viewing Ronald Ong's Heights

Clouds are the opposite of a magnifying glass
frying ants and browning grass
beneath.

Yet more than mere shadow,
    a light-blot freckling terrain
    or less: mere wisp on the vault

    pressed against sky in hide and seek,
    peeking at horizons
    for the space station;

is when they rally, mob a shire,
fog-squat, squall in picket lines,
defy visibility.

That shadow one makes
cools, mutates,
mirrors effect less appearance

of a fleecy mist spot,

a roaming temperature drop,

one side sunning itself in careless backstroke

until caught by a tree

like a giant cotton shrub,

then sipped by a giraffe.

Marble Caves

The Marble Caves nest in a lake, rock texture streaky, lit with bent rays through blue swash sparkled with glacier particles.

Waves spill then disgorge from the many mouths, oval open, whoosh and cluck acoustics polyphonic through fluted hollows—not siren song but hungry chicks, throats marine-bright and cartilage-ringed.

If this were a cut geode I would plunge in liquid quartz, plumb deep one cobalt call to find fossil brachiopods in limestone drill-core.

They tempted me in the Kimberley, all the way from Devonian era reefs, stone-blue shells a meal withheld while I logged kilometres of them for months. They had one name. I recorded their existence, humpbacked and footsore. Every minute a repetition of their last moments.

They were singly steamed or they partied in clusters, prep bowls at a long table. They imprinted my dreams, hopping in flurries, like grasshopper plagues after a big wet, among rotten-egg gas plumes hissing from mud pots, to sauté into an acid lake.

There I dipped, carefully, stagnant limbs so corrosive words dissolved any mould. Mildewed beliefs and fingerprints boiled in a fizz just toxic enough for something to prove. This was not the Elixir of Life, but surely part of it. If I were clever enough to find the rest, would I even need it?

With waters neutralised by limestone and old lies, I plunged in, to wash up on a black-sand beach salted with ice chunks. Footfalls crunched, whooping gusts made ninja stars of tiny snow crystals and the sea chinkle-swept more diamond lumps—my name etched in each one. It seems new environments brought more range to my survival, despite feeling awry.

The wind struck the rims of icy concavities, bowled fragments of tonal whispers. Strung together: *Our iceberg says to dive deeper.*

Nudibranchs

Somewhere a sea creature
takes weapons of prey
for itself

and wolfs jellyfish, stingers first
for fire-ready barbs
quill-patterned on its back.

The chemical defence
of sponges renders inedible
their klepto-venomed predator.

Soft-coral's pigments
absorb as neon cautions:
tattooed phosphorescence

(as if a feud between a sea god
and a bead-glassblower's muse
romped through a florist's shop).

The little warriors, sea slugs,
benthic, photogenic
with thorns, frills, feathery tufts,

frippery, pops of colour
make arsenals an art. Unbothered
by ocean photographers,

a charm in sashayed promenade,
essence of the adage to never arm
those who won't learnt to dance

they pageant their attitude:
you are what you eat
so be that, and feast.

G-force Nine

Merry-go-round to apoplectic sky,
I'm flung over a towered wave fierce
to impassive, flint-faced cliffs.
Past the roaring lip, I pierce
ocean's hushed opaque skin
to cubic clarity.
Below that empty fathom
I fall through successions
of unknowns at pressures
so the heart convulses,
mind extinguished.
Then a pause
to teleport again another life.

        Blocks away, wind tickles a gum tree.
        Hello, old friend. The torus whirls
        from my crown to topiary,
        down heartwood, through earth
        a thousand filaments hold
        tiny versions of us, or link other trees,

on the looping route to my feet.
G-force 9: merge into my mango's trunk
appear at the gum. Then back again.
Press between the brows,
appear in frigid fog where
Yakushima's climates force
decay-resistant resin stores.
Giant daisugi cedar scaffolds
its thin straight shoots
scaled and pruned
by harvesters inheriting
new timber for centuries—
flexible, unblemished, strong—
from one anchored, unfelled vault.
Its shape suggests a paling fence
in wreathing forest;
baleen bristles on whale jaw
a fist of straws drinking light
or slim fingers and flat palm
over gnarled wrist:
a living, steady reach for infinity.

Collar bells and sun-sieve leaves,
dirt-pocked paths in crunch-struck snow:
reindeer mine for lichen.
In different worlds, any one of these
is me. Fixed in earth, with angel-shields
I Christmas star: burst light
to every multiversal self.
Beyond the speed
that atomizes matter,
graduate 3D and nothing lies too far.
We express in fields of forces,
travel in arcs,
draw in our brightest mystery.

Dracaena Cinnabari

Socotra island births dragon-blood trees;
crimp-limbed branches cradle bladed leaves
by views of the prismatic Arabian sea.

They grow slow in drought with leaf tips up-turned
to trickle in vertical rare sip-sky dew:
a thin crystal vein from forked branch to roots.

They hold their heads high over bird-sown seeds;
bathe mercy on thin soil and bare stone: they sweep
their day-crept silhouette's glare-cut relief.

They're blood-let and scarred for their fabulous resin
for poetry, magic and demon deterrent,
abortions and fevers. Violin varnish.

Their roots mine limestone's sea-creature tombs,
crack cement corpses, pump arid juice
with spectres of water in heat-rippled noons.

They cry carmine sap for their cemetery island,
throw back their mushroom-cut manes, delighted
they'd mastered outlasting in drip-fed defiance.

Lighting Incense to Ancestors

One ember offers a heat-stem,
opaque air fights clear currents
that scribble the ribbon then topple
slowed dispersing smoke
into wushu flows. Wings unfurl, invert:
falcons flown from Mongolian horsemen
or dust plumes by spectral hooves?
Vapor-color bleeds a whorled tongue:
sandalwood and frangipani
with nasal singe-bitter tinge
sharpens my faith in the substance
of this connection.

Great-grandmother Hoy Foong Saow
staked billowing reeds, by trees
and good rocks, for the god of that tree
and this rock with prayers, gratitude
and an almond eye for beauty.
At temple she veiled thick, from bad spirits,
in sandalwood's scent-shield.
Now, she swathes a presence

in bone-bound court of ancients
and guardians; gauze conversations
loop and sign between
my living and my dead.

In this country, I've forgotten
the obligations: a vague list:
the altar, don't wash hair
on the Water God's birthday,
spring clean before Lunar New Year,
and reverent Tao. More relevant
a sufficient religion
shrugs ghosts off masala resin's
straight brown finger's burning point
evoking wood dust, tea and a brief pass
through Indian hands rolling
the wands to translation.

In rekindled muscle twitch
lives rites. A thousand forebears copied
in this act of spark and ceremony.
Many contemporaries bring our DNA's
people, travel, trauma,

glories, flaws and skills
to mind with a lit stick.
Our generational jaunt, too,
will smooth into a fumbling whisp;
our stories become lived proverbs
made pure oil, kindling
and fragrant ash.

The Beaches Parkrun, Australia, December

Trailing the pack, a head start
on my resolutions, faltering
—unseasonal squalls
punch buoyant anticipation
down to stern participation—

> but bolstered by the festive foam,
> a white Christmas from the sea god,
> and tossed about in the spume:
> a kite-surfer grapples
> with grim thrills.

Calves whine of sunk treads,
tricky depths in channel froth
high-stepped.
Big toes flick grit-balls;
I puff louder than the bluster.

> I smile at how ridiculous
> is this stupid Parkrun
> for the goal of a saltwater dip

>   (inconceivable below 40 °C
>   hence earned with a sweat)
>   miscalculated by 30 knots.

Front runners turn back to cruise the next lap
and on display I feign a gallop.
Whipping winds peel my lips
to grin at the insult
of a halfway flag.

Now the knots swing the soles, a charm at my back
—no cat o'nine gales—
home banners bounce closer

> *Every effort is a choice*
> *about who you are*
> I roll my eyes
> I haven't yet chosen to stop
> so I do not.

> *I don't vomit while running anymore,*
> I say at the grave of a sergeant
> buried decades in my psyche,

but since I am here,
I may as well enjoy
whatever tries to kill me

and come back next week.

www.ingramcontent.com/pod-product-compliance
Lightning Source LLC
Chambersburg PA
CBHW051956290426
44110CB00015B/2264